Duffy's Iowa Caucus Cartoons

Iowa and the Midwest Experience

William B. Friedricks, series editor

Iowa History Center at Simpson College

DUFFY'S

IOWA CAUCUS CARTOONS

Watch 'Em Run

Brian Duffy

Foreword by David Yepsen

UNIVERSITY OF IOWA PRESS • IOWA CITY

University of Iowa Press, Iowa City 52242

www.uiowapress.org
Printed in the United States of America

Design by April Leidig

Cartoons courtesy of *Des Moines Register.*

The University of Iowa Press is a member of Green Press Initiative and is committed to preserving natural resources.

Printed on acid-free paper

Library of Congress Cataloging-in-Publication Data
Duffy, Brian, 1955– author
Duffy's Iowa caucus cartoons : watch 'em run / Brian Duffy ; foreword by David Yepsen.
Pages cm.—(Iowa and the Midwest Experience)
978-1-60938-379-4 (pbk), ISBN 978-1-60938-380-0 (ebk)
1. Primaries—Iowa—History—Caricatures and cartoons.
2. Presidents—United States—Nomination—History—Caricatures and cartoons. I. Title.
JK2075.I82D84 2016
324.273'1520977709045—dc23 2015017225

For my daughters,
Tara, Shanna, Tiffin, and Alissa

Contents

Foreword

BY DAVID YEPSEN

For years, one of Brian Duffy's caucus cartoon trademarks has been pigs. Iowans have smiled at the pigs' wry comments over the fence, one hog to another, about presidential candidates or newsies traipsing about the state. Or a pack of hogs might be used as stand-ins for the pack of candidates in Iowa.

The porkers are just one of the metaphors Duffy has used to brighten the days of many Iowans. Sometimes his targets haven't found the cartoonist too funny, but they get over it. After all, as the saying goes, "tomorrow is another day," and hopefully there's another Duffy illustration to ease the pain of its news.

With this volume we get a nice fix of Duffy cartoons, just in time to lighten the load of another presidential campaign.

I worked at the *Des Moines Register* when Duffy first started. Over the years, we shared a passion for politics. We split on the question of bike rides across Iowa, however. (He loved them. I couldn't stand the events, which is why my knees are intact. The only time I ever saw Duffy get mad was when I told him the bike rides were a good idea because they kept bicycles away from the front of my SUV.)

Still, the bike was often as much a part of his work as the pigs.

Early in his term as governor of Iowa, I don't think Terry Branstad appreciated Duffy's characterization of him as a little squirt. In one, a kid was facing Democratic street toughs in a "well, if it isn't the little governor" cartoon. A while after one of those characterizations of Branstad appeared, I happened to be in the family home interviewing his mother only to notice a copy of the cartoon stuck on the refrigerator. (Moms are like that.) She loved it so much it merited a place of honor on the family fridge.

Duffy is always an equal opportunity "skewerer"; at one time or another, most major politicians get a turn on the spit. Even though some of them hate it, more than once I had some pol pull me aside and ask, "Hey, can you get a copy of that Duffy cartoon?" "You mean that one portraying you as a numbskull?" "Yeah!"

What Duffy could do with his work was give voice to what many people felt: anger at something stupid, outrage at someone corrupt, or the pain we feel during a time of tragedy.

I spent most of my career at the *Des Moines Register* covering politics, which I consider the only game for adults because the stakes are so high. In Iowa, covering—and illustrating—politics means presidential politics. The Iowa caucuses have been a significant part of the nation's presidential selection process since the early 1970s.

The caucuses as a test of strength were born out of the Vietnam War protests. In 1968, the Democratic National Convention in Chicago was disrupted by anti-war protesters. Police overreaction to the demonstrators became the story and marred the party's image. Many experts believe Vice President Hubert Humphrey's narrow loss to former Vice President Richard Nixon occurred because the convention troubles alienated many southern and blue-collar Democrats.

Those events and that outcome prompted party leaders—particularly those on the left like Iowa governor Harold Hughes—to argue the party needed to open itself up to people, to hear their concerns and let them have a say in nominees and platforms. A commission was formed, and one conclusion was the party should make the selection of national convention delegates a more open process. Instead of courting party bosses and elites, presidential candidates should court rank-and-file party members.

In Iowa, reform Democrats concluded there should be more time between various stages of the delegate selection process. If the national convention was to be held in August, then giving people time to mount campaigns for delegates or draft platform resolutions would mean the state convention would need to be held in June. If the state convention were held in June, congressional district conventions needed to be in May. If congressional district conventions were to be in May, then county conventions had to be in March. That meant precinct caucuses needed to be held in February.

Party staffers of that era, like Richard Bender and Barry Piatt, say one reason the party spread out the events was because that was how fast their old Gestetner mimeograph machine could print proposed platform resolutions and other party paperwork.

While there have been precinct caucuses in Iowa for decades, they just didn't have the limelight on them as they did after these changes. (Lex Hawkins, a longtime party leader, said, "We thought it was a reform when we told people where the caucuses were.") Now, Iowa was a lead-off state.

Of course, all that meant Iowa would start selecting delegates to the national convention earlier than any other state. (One reason Hughes and his friends liked the idea of early caucuses wasn't because of some old mimeograph machine but because he was considering a run for the White House himself in 1972. He eventually dropped that idea.)

In 1972, South Dakota senator George McGovern and his campaign manager, Gary Hart, lit upon the idea of making an early stand in Iowa against the front runner, Maine senator Edmund Muskie. McGovern finished a surprise second. He beat what he was expected to do, which is the media definition of "news." It was chronicled by a dozen or so reporters who made the trek to Iowa to cover the events. After McGovern went on to win the nomination that year, reporters decided that the caucus events did, in fact, say something about the outcome of the race.

That fact wasn't lost on Georgia governor Jimmy Carter, who quietly started campaigning in Iowa for the Democratic nomination in 1976. Other candidates followed, and Carter's victory in Iowa—"undecided" actually finished first, but Carter got more votes than the other candidates—gave him a big boost of media attention. After he won the White House, the importance of the caucus events was cemented. On the Republican side that year, governor of California Ronald Reagan's close finish against

President Gerald Ford presaged their spirited contest for the nomination which Ford won, albeit in a weakened fashion that led to his defeat in November.

In 1980, the Democratic caucuses were the battlefield for the famous Jimmy Carter versus Massachusetts senator Edward Kennedy contest. The Republican side saw Director of the Central Intelligence Agency George H. W. Bush emerge from obscurity with a victory, one that led to his battle with Reagan and the consolation prize of being Reagan's running mate.

That year also saw Tennessee senator Howard Baker finish third, and he famously said, "Iowa winnows the field and I've been winnowed in."

The three roles Iowa plays in the presidential selection process were now set: (1) some candidates win and are slingshot into victories in other states; (2) other candidates do well enough—are winnowed in—to be able to continue to fight on in other states; (3) then there are those candidates who do poorly—who see their momentum and their money dry up—and are winnowed out.

All this meant the role of New Hampshire as the first state in the process had changed. The Iowa caucus results were important because they affected the outcome of the New Hampshire primary. (The two states quit fighting with each other over who went first in 1983 when it was decided Iowa would have the first caucus and New Hampshire the first primary, and instead of fighting between themselves they'd fight together to fend off other states that wanted to poach.)

Other states, jealous of all this attention, have tried for years to find a way to knock Iowa out of its first-in-the-nation role. They've failed because while many dislike the presidential selection process in the United States, they can't agree on a way to change it. Political inertia keeps the caucuses alive.

Today, caucus events are huge. They are so large they have lost much of their small-town charm. Instead of meeting people in living rooms the way Jimmy Carter did, campaigns rent school auditoriums. Reporters don't hop in the back seat with a candidate like they did in the old days; now, they pack press buses.

The media crush grows larger each cycle as new technologies enable more people to cover the events on more platforms. Candidates see the media and come to Iowa. In turn, the media see candidates and come to cover them. Chicken or egg, anyone?

While Iowa is still an important early test, the first big test of a campaign is the money primary. The old days in which an underfunded candidate could win Iowa and parlay that victory into money and media attention are gone. The old days in which a candidate could try out themes and ideas in someone's kitchen have vanished, too.

Today, a serious candidate better show up in Iowa ready for prime time and with millions in the till. A lack of money means a lack of media and staff organizers. A fumbling answer can spell the death of a campaign because every word uttered is instantly broadcast and tweeted around the world.

Critics of this process say it gives Iowa too much influence over the nomination. They also note Iowa is predominantly white and rural, which makes it atypical of the rest of the country. (That fact proved useful to Illinois senator Barack Obama in 2008 after he won Iowa, convincing doubters—particularly some African Americans—that he could carry white votes.)

Over time, the two major parties have responded to criticisms by working to ensure the integrity of the process and the tabulation of the votes. National parties have also brought South Carolina and Nevada into the rank of the early contests, a move that means one small state in the Midwest, one in New England, one in the South and one in the West have important early voices in who the nominees are.

Critics of the nomination process say these early states empower the most extreme, activist elements in each party. In the GOP, the caucuses are dominated by social conservatives. In the Democratic party, labor unions and left-of-center groups hold sway. These critics point out that this process pulls nominees too far to one extreme or the other, making it difficult for them to win the main event in November when a larger, more centrist electorate is being courted.

Yet the types of people who show up at caucuses tend to look like the folks who wind up on the floor of each national convention. So guess what? The Republican National Convention is dominated by religious conservatives, and Democrats have heavy influence from liberals and labor. While Iowa's caucuses don't reflect the nation as a whole, they do reflect the sorts of people who are active in each party.

All that background is important for putting Duffy's work in context. Caucus events are media events. They attract some pretty far-out views. They attract hordes of media and special interest groups and, yes, caucus tourists who come to the state to get their own up-close look at the candidates. The caucuses have an impact on Iowa politics after the campaigns leave the state. The campaigns take over Iowa airwaves, media, and politics for months in advance. They are the stage for famous mistakes and gaffes by candidates.

You'll see those sorts of events displayed in Duffy's work.

Sometimes with two pigs talking about them.

Duffy’s Iowa Caucus Cartoons

Introduction

IT IS NOTHING out of the ordinary for a candidate to sit down with members of the editorial department of a newspaper. They are used to interacting with the writers, editors, photographers, and videographers, but toss a cartoonist into the mix and they don't know what to think. When I was working for the *Des Moines Register* I would attend the presidential candidate forums and cart along a pad of paper and pencils to sketch my impression of them. This was disconcerting to more than a few of them. Presidential candidate Barack Obama complained, "You guys always draw my ears too big." I told him he should have seen what I did to businessman and 1992 presidential candidate Ross Perot.

Virtually every major party candidate since 1983 who has marked time in Iowa has been recorded from my drawing board. I've captured almost every success, surprise, blooper, and blunder with pen and ink. The Iowa Caucuses are still considered the starting line in the race for the White House, and despite continuous efforts to get rid of them, they survive, and so do I.

Iowa, the Caucuses, and a Little Bit of History about Both

The state is named for the Ioway Indian tribe that used to inhabit the state. Actually, the name comes from the French word for the tribe, which is *aiouez*, meaning "sleepy people." The Iowa legislature thought better of naming the state after a tribe of narcoleptics, so they changed the meaning of the word to "beautiful land." Iowa is also known as the Land between Two Rivers, the Tall Corn State, the Hawkeye State, and the Terrytory of Branstad, in honor of the man who has been governor since the "sleepy people" owned the land.

The term "caucus" is thought to have originated in North America. The when, where, and why are still open to discussion. One story goes that it came from Boston's shipbuilding district in the 1770s where rope makers and caulkers held secret meetings to discuss plans for rebellion against England. So how do you get from caulkers to caucus? Well, you have to be familiar with the "Bahhhstin" accent to know that inhabitants of this area have lost the ability to pronounce the sound of the letter R, which comes out sounding like "ahh," hence, "caulkers" becomes "cawwkahhs." From there, it's not too far a stretch to get to caucus.

Okay, maybe it is. The more accepted theory is that the word came from the Algonquin noun *caucauasu*, meaning "one who advises or encourages."

Put the two words together and once again the meaning is open to interpretation. For instance, former *Des Moines Register* columnist Donald Kaul referred to the caucuses as a "nice little oddball event." A former presidential candidate considers the caucuses akin to the La Brea Tar Pits: "No one comes out the way they went in."

Close to 90 percent of the state's land is used to grow corn and soybeans and raise chickens, cattle, hogs, and—every four years—presidential candidates.

The political term "testing the waters" takes on a completely new meaning in Iowa (here for Massachusetts governor Michael Dukakis, the 1988 Democratic candidate).

Iowa has close to 450 different soil types, enough to satisfy the most discriminating mudslinger. Front: former Massachusetts governor Mitt Romney and Arizona senator John McCain, Republicans; back: Illinois senator Barack Obama and New York senator Hillary Clinton, Democrats.

RAGBRAI—the Register's Annual Great Bicycle Ride Across Iowa—draws close to 15,000 cyclists to the state every July. Wherever you find a crowd, you can bet there's a politician or two lurking nearby. The following presidential aspirants have been spotted on the ride over the years: Secretary of the Interior Bruce Babbitt, Secretary of State John Kerry, businessman Steve Forbes, Tennessee senator Lamar Alexander, and North Carolina senator John Edwards, who was spotted tooling down the road with Lance Armstrong.

Over 3,000 members of the media cover the Iowa Caucuses, and they all seem to know the best restaurants in the state.

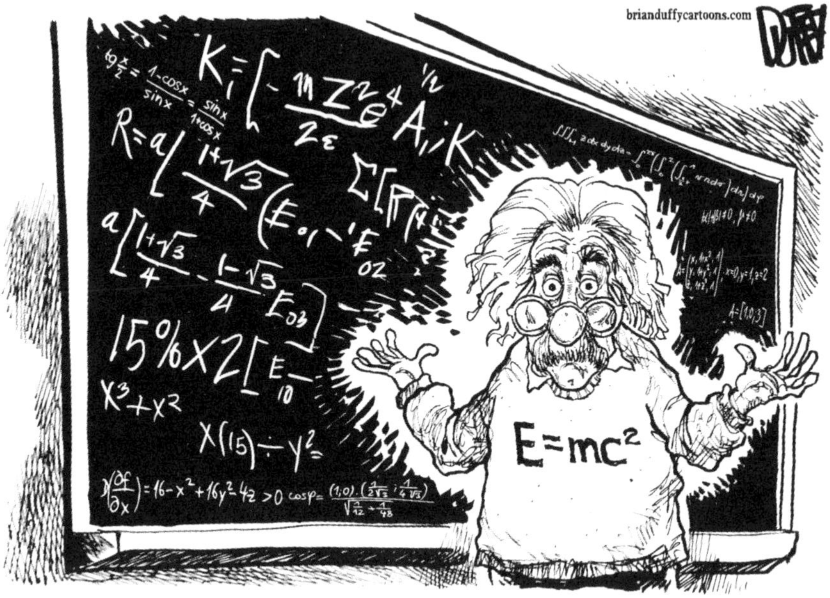

The nominating process: both political parties hold caucuses on the same night, usually the coldest and/or snowiest night of the year. For the Republicans, the first order of business is the selection of county committee officers and county convention delegates. Next, slips of paper are handed out and the Republicans write down their choice of a presidential candidate. The ballots are collected, counted, and the totals reported to the state party, whose job it is to forward that information on to the media. And that's it! You're done and you can go outside and wait for the tow truck to come and jump your car's frozen battery.

The procedures for the Democratic caucus are completely different and more time consuming, so it's recommended that you bring along a pillow and blanket. The first order of business is to elect a chairperson and a secretary. Next, the participants are required to sit patiently for a half hour before they can start forming preference groups. Anybody caught starting before the whistle is blown is disqualified. When the game begins, groups backing the same candidate stake out a territory in the room. Then they name their piece of the room something like "Hillary's Village." The chairperson counts the total number of people in the room and then the number in each group to determine which groups are "viable" and which are not. The viability threshold is set at 15 percent of the total number of participants. If a preference group falls below 15 percent, it has thirty minutes to become viable.

What follows is a grand game of Red Rover during which viable and nonviable groups attempt to cajole, bribe, or kidnap members of nonviable groups. When time is up, those remaining in nonviable groups are lined up for their last shot at viability in the Lightning Round. Those that remain nonviable are out of the game. A numerical value based on a proportion of allotted delegates is given to each viable group. This number is sent to the party headquarters and reported to the media. Then the caucus participants regroup, elect county central committee members, and debate platform resolutions; all this is done before the sun comes up.

The Republicans add up the cumulative votes per candidate by precinct and report that number. The Democrats use a more complicated mathematical formula (Fermat's Second to Last Theorem) for assigning a number to their candidates.

Iowa law requires a thirty-day period between each of the four steps in the process leading from the precinct caucus to the national conventions. The interval is necessary in order to gather the names of delegates and platform resolutions and get them all copied. Thirty days. It seems that neither party is aware of the invention of moveable type, even though there is a town in the state named after its inventor.

And if that is what it takes to keep Iowa first, I think it's worth it, don't you?

1976

IN 1972, BUILDING on changes to party rules between 1968 and 1972, the Democratic Party moved its Iowa precinct caucuses up to January 24, making it the first such event in the nation. This schedule also meant that the Iowa caucuses happened before the New Hampshire primary election, which had traditionally been the first primary to occur each election year. In 1976, Iowa Republicans agreed with Democrats to hold their caucuses on the same date to maximize national media attention, and the parties have continued to do so ever since. Other states frequently try to preempt or diminish the outsize role that Iowa and New Hampshire—two lightly populated, disproportionately rural and white states—play in the presidential elections. Iowa and New Hampshire have scrambled to maintain their status.

In 1976, the presidential candidates and the media were only slowly realizing the new importance of Iowa in the campaign for the White House. Democratic candidate Jimmy Carter, the governor of Georgia, first showed what a difference success here could make. He was largely unknown in the state at the start of his campaign. Famously, at one of his first events in the state, he ordered food and drink for hundreds—and only three people showed up. At the press conference that followed, only the *Des Moines Register*'s David Yepsen showed up. He and Carter sat down and ate grapes together. Eventually, Carter's persistent campaigning paid off.

Among the other Democratic candidates were Minnesota senator Hubert Humphrey, Senator Birch Bayh of Indiana, Sargent Shriver (a statesman during the Kennedy and Johnson administrations and former Peace Corps director), Washington senator Henry Jackson, Congressman Morris Udall of Arizona, and Oklahoma senator Fred Harris. Carter claimed victory in the end, though he was outpolled by "uncommitted." On the Republican side, incumbent president Gerald Ford faced an unexpected challenge from California governor Ronald Reagan, but neither campaigned in Iowa. Ultimately, Carter bested Ford to take the White House.

Few Iowans knew Jimmy Carter going into the presidential race, but since he had chaired the Democratic Governors' Campaign Committee and the Democratic National Campaign Committee, he had support in the national Democratic Party. Following Watergate and the Vietnam War, voters responded positively to his slogan "A Leader, for a Change."

Though Carter was the top vote-getter among the Democratic candidates, he was outpolled by "uncommitted," 37.2 percent to 27.6 percent. None of the other candidates reached the 15 percent viability standard, so he was the only candidate awarded delegates.

1980

BY 1980 ALL OF THE candidates recognized that they had to campaign in Iowa, and they launched their efforts well before the caucuses. Among the Republicans, California governor Ronald Reagan was the early front runner; also running were Texas congressman George H. W. Bush, Tennessee senator Howard Baker, former secretary of the treasury John Connally, Illinois congressman Phillip Crane, Illinois congressman John Anderson, and Kansas senator Bob Dole. Learning from sitting president Jimmy Carter's experience in 1976, Bush crisscrossed the state meeting with people while Reagan barely campaigned in Iowa at all. Bush took top honors, with Reagan close behind—later, Reagan would thank Iowans for giving him the necessary "kick in the pants" that propelled him to victory in the primaries. Among the Democrats, Massachusetts senator Ted Kennedy challenged Carter, but his lack of success in Iowa undermined his campaign. In the presidential election in the fall, Reagan defeated Carter by a landslide.

Reagan had a history with Iowa. He had been a sports announcer for WHO radio in Des Moines back in the 1930s and had received 43 percent of the votes in the 1976 Iowa caucuses, just 2 percentage points behind President Ford. So it was a mystery to many Iowans why he was ignoring the state this time around.

Reagan didn't pay attention to the sound of the footsteps coming up from behind him. They weren't hard to miss, either. George H. W. Bush had stomped his way to wins in one preference poll after another, including the much-hyped Ames Straw Poll.

1984

THANKS TO MORE changes in party rules, states began moving their caucus or primary events earlier in the year. However, candidates continued to take Iowa very seriously; some had begun visiting the state as early as 1982. The leading Democrat was Minnesota senator and former vice president Walter "Fritz" Mondale; also running were California senator Alan Cranston, Senator Gary Hart of Colorado, former astronaut and Ohio senator John Glenn, Florida governor Reubin Askew, South Carolina senator Ernest Hollings, civil rights activist Reverend Jesse Jackson, and South Dakota senator George McGovern. The caucus results gave Mondale a big win, as expected, with Hart and McGovern taking second and third. Saying of Iowa "You can get awful famous in this country in seven days," Hart leveraged his second-place finish to a victory in the New Hampshire primary. Little activity occurred on the Republican side, as incumbent president Ronald Reagan was running unchallenged for reelection. Reagan would be returned to office for a second term in the November election.

President Reagan famously asked Americans if they were better off after his first term in office. With no opponent in the primary, he did not campaign in Iowa prior to the caucuses.

A series of nonbinding straw polls in California, Maine, Massachusetts, and Wisconsin left the Democratic candidates scrambling for a good showing so that they would be well-positioned going into the Iowa caucuses. Left: Hart, Cranston, Hollings, Mondale, Glenn, McGovern, Askew.

Walter Mondale, the front runner and eventual winner of the Iowa Poll, ran on a traditional New-Deal–style platform.

Glenn skipped a farm policy debate at Iowa State University to go on a fund-raising run through the South. Of all the candidates I have drawn, Glenn was the toughest to caricature. All I can say is that I thank my lucky stars he was an astronaut.

The Jefferson-Jackson Day Dinner is the Iowa Democratic Party's yearly fundraiser. In 1983, it drew close to 6,000 people to listen to speeches by seven presidential candidates. By luck of the draw, Mondale spoke last and tore into Glenn, his main rival, for voting in favor of Reagan's tax cuts. For his part, Glenn had criticized Mondale for being a tool of special interests.

There are certain things Iowans can count on when it comes to the weather: snowstorms during the girls' high school basketball tournament and conditions fit for neither man nor beast on caucus night.

The Iowa caucuses are an expectation game; candidates may exceed or disappoint expectations, but they rarely meet them. Glenn's problem was that his own campaign fell short, while Mondale's met its expectations. Glenn finished sixth in the caucuses and never recovered.

Love is a two-way relationship: if a candidate gets some, he is expected to give some in return.

Glenn pulled the plug on his campaign on March 16, shortly after his losses in several southern primaries. At that point, he had won less than 4 percent of the primary votes nationwide. He had the vehicle: he was a fighter pilot, a test pilot, an astronaut, a business leader, and a senator—"the Right Stuff." But he lacked the fuel: a political platform and charisma. In Iowa, if you're not on the launch pad when the countdown starts, you're out of luck.

1988

FOR THE FIRST TIME since 1972, there was no sitting president running for reelection, so both the Republicans and the Democrats campaigned vigorously in Iowa. The farm crisis had weakened the state's economy and put its citizens in a sour mood, making the Democrats hope they could reclaim the White House from the Republicans. Eight men contested the Democratic nomination: Missouri congressman Dick Gephardt, Colorado senator Gary Hart, the Reverend Jesse Jackson, Delaware senator Joe Biden, former Arizona governor Bruce Babbitt (who launched his campaign by riding in the *Register*'s Annual Great Bicycle Race Across Iowa, or RAGBRAI), Illinois senator Paul Simon, Massachusetts governor Michael Dukakis, and Tennessee senator Al Gore Jr.

The Republicans also fielded eight candidates: Vice President George H. W. Bush, former Kansas senator Bob Dole, Christian broadcaster and activist Pat Robertson, New York congressman and former professional football player Jack Kemp, former Delaware governor Pete DuPont, former secretary of defense Donald Rumsfeld, former secretary of state Alexander Haig, and former Nevada senator Paul Laxalt. Only the first five campaigned actively, and overall the Republicans spent less time and money in Iowa than the Democrats.

Among the Democrats, Gephardt won the caucuses, with Simon and Dukakis taking second and third; among the Republicans, Dole finished first, with Robertson and Bush following in that order. The third-place finishers became the nominees for both parties, with Bush defeating Dukakis in the November election.

Famous last words of Gary Hart: “Follow me around. I don’t care. I’m serious. If anybody wants to put a tail on me, go ahead. They’d be very bored.” They did and they weren’t.

The Seven Dwarfs of the Iowa caucuses were a group of unknown Lilliputians, none of whom managed to crack double digits in any poll. This group included Jackson, Gephardt, Babbitt, Dukakis, Biden, Gore, and Simon. Playing the part of Snow White was Gary Hart, who was photographed in a compromising situation aboard a boat aptly named "Monkey Business" and headed home to Troublesome Gulch, which is a real place (besides being a frame of mind).

Pat Robertson told the media that he would run for the presidency only if he received the “okay” from the Big Guy upstairs.

Haig announced his intentions to run for the Republican nomination in 1988. At least that's what people thought he said. Haig's speeches tended toward "polysyllabic fog."

Gore chose to skip Iowa and focus on the Super Tuesday states down south instead. As he explained, "If you're going duck hunting, you go where the ducks are; if you're going delegate hunting, you go where the delegates are." And if you're looking to get your campaign off the ground, you come to Iowa.

Biden was on a roll until he was flagged for unsportsmanlike conduct. A video replay showed him plagiarizing a speech by British Labour Party leader Neil Kinnock.

It was discovered that the Dukakis campaign furnished the incriminating Biden tape.

From "Big Mo" in 1980 to laid low in 1988. George H. W. Bush had won every informal straw poll prior to the 1980 caucuses, even beating front runner Reagan by 25 percentage points at that year's iteration of the Ames "Cavalcade of Stars" fundraiser. What a difference eight years made when Robertson and a cadre of evangelical outriders ambushed him in front of 200 credentialed reporters.

The ambush was enough to scare the trunks off of GOP investors nationally.

He's Back! Four months after exiling himself to Troublesome Gulch, Gary Hart reappeared on the campaign trail. His return shoved the remaining six striving dwarfs off center stage. Unanswered questions included where would he get the money to run, especially since he was still in debt from his 1984 campaign. And what about Donna Rice, the woman with whom he'd been accused of having an extramarital affair? His answer to that seemed like a prequel to President Bill Clinton's "It depends on what your definition of 'is' is" during the congressional hearings about his relationship with White House employee Monica Lewinsky.

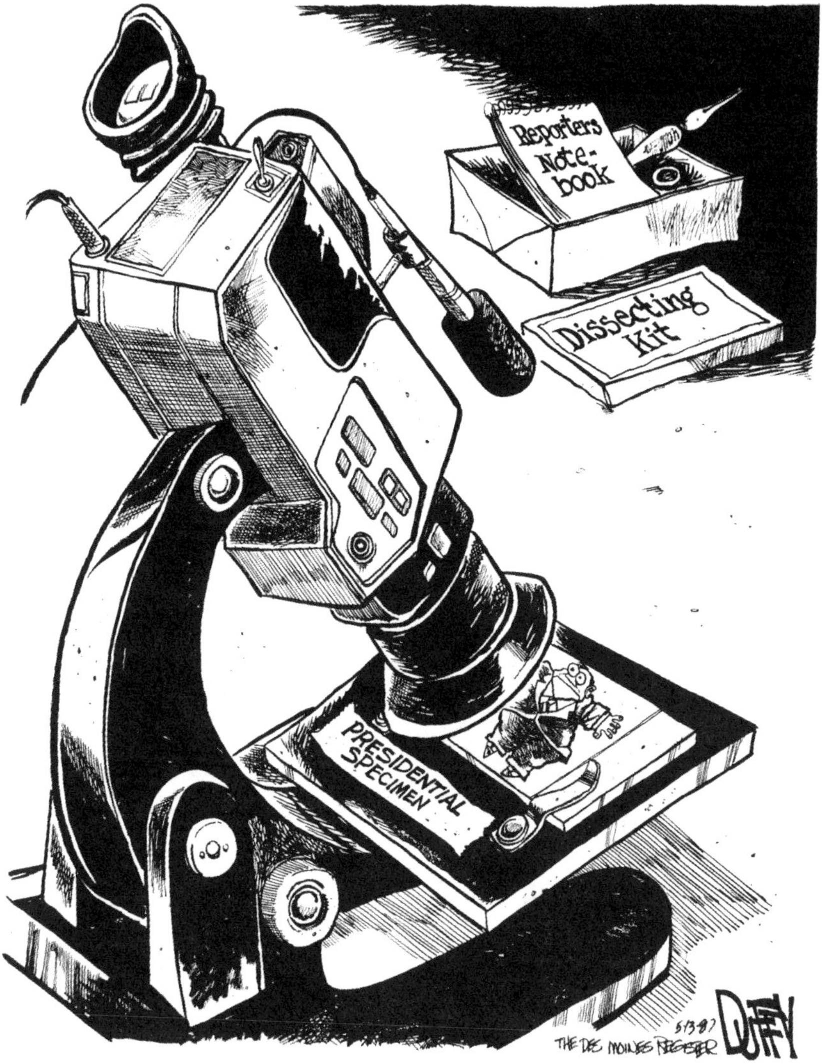

The events of this caucus year showed that if an individual had designs on the White House, then he had better be prepared to have their life dissected down to the cellular level.

Dukakis seemed to lack the requisite fire in the belly, giving his staff indigestion.

Dole excelled at getting under an opponent's skin. He put Bush in a real tizzy by playing the class warfare card to perfection, reminding audiences that he grew up poor in tiny Russell, Kansas, during the 1930s Dust Bowl—light years away from the upper-crust east coast society that was so familiar to Bush.

Eight years prior, Bush had slapped that label on Reagan's supply-side economics idea that tax cuts would lead to increased tax revenue. After two terms swallowing the Kool-Aid as Reagan's vice president, he came up with his own flavor to peddle.

HOME STRETCH

With five weeks to go, Gephardt narrowed his message down to two issues, trade and farming, and pulled away down the backstretch. Mounted on his Missouri mule, Gephardt crossed the line first, winning sixty of ninety-nine Iowa counties.

THE BURNING BUSH

It had yet to be proven if Robertson could walk on water, but he did know how to burn a Bush. His second-place finish in the caucuses surprised just about everybody, particularly the vice president who had won the event back in 1980.

At the stroke of midnight after the caucuses, Iowa turned back into a pumpkin and some of the less successful candidates turned into, well, whatever they were before.

So how did the winners of the 1988 Iowa caucuses make out? Well, that's disappointing.

1992

THE CAUCUS CAMPAIGN season grew steadily longer between 1972 and 1988, but in 1992 it was cut short by the Persian Gulf War and President George H. W. Bush's enormous popularity. As candidates and media neglected Iowa, the Democratic and Republican parties—as well as hotels and restaurants—felt the pinch of lost business. Meanwhile, other states began another effort to unseat Iowa from its place as the nation's first caucus.

Looking at Bush's sky-high poll numbers, leading Democrats declined to seek their party's nomination, leaving the field open for dark horse candidates. Among the long shots who decided to take a chance were Nebraska senator Bob Kerrey, former Massachusetts senator Paul Tsongas, Virginia governor Douglas Wilder, Iowa senator Tom Harkin, Arkansas governor Bill Clinton, former California governor Jerry Brown. Given Harkin's favored-son status, the media largely wrote off the Iowa results; indeed, Harkin won more than two-thirds of the delegates, leaving his rivals in the dust.

The state Republicans decided not to hold caucuses since neither President Bush nor his challenger (conservative commentator Pat Buchanan) campaigned in Iowa. In November, Bush lost to Clinton, and the Democrats retook the White House.

Bush started his reelection campaign in form as fine as basketball superstar Michael Jordan in early 1991. Following the end of the Persian Gulf War, a Gallup Poll showed his approval ratings at 89 percent, the highest of any president since 1945. The big question was his hang time.

Thanks to Bush's popularity, none of the Democrats generally considered political heavyweights—including Missouri congressman Richard Gephardt, West Virginia senator John D. ("Jay") Rockefeller, Texas senator Lloyd Bentsen, and New York governor Mario Cuomo—were interested in running.

The annual migration has been called off due to lack of interest.

Cue the theme from *Jaws*. Harkin indicated that he was exploring the idea of running for president, not long after winning reelection, a feat no other Iowa Democrat had accomplished.

When Harkin announced his intentions to run, the Iowa caucuses joined the Maytag Repairman as the loneliest folks in town.

In announcing his candidacy, Harkin made it clear that he intended to spur the party hard left, returning to an activist role for government.

In the tradition of "give 'em hell" President Harry Truman, Harkin's response to Bush's economic policies—and his rallying cry—was "bullshit." It was not well received in some circles.

It was an easy mistake to make: former Minnesota governor Harold Stassen had run for president nine times. South Dakota senator George McGovern was considering what would be his fourth run since his upset win in the 1972 Democratic presidential primaries.

Third-party candidate and businessman Ross Perot made his supporters dizzy by his on-again, off-again campaign. In the end, he was one of the most successful third-party candidates in U.S. history, winning nearly 19 percent of the popular vote.

What goes up must come down, and this is particularly true for presidents seeking a second term. Bush plummeted down to earth, going from one of the highest presidential approval ratings ever to one of the lowest—29 percent—in a little over a year, largely thanks to worsening economic conditions and an unpopular tax increase.

A weak field of candidates too reticent even to announce their candidacies until the fall of 1991 left the Democratic Party in search of a savior. When Cuomo began dropping hints that he might be interested, they thought they had found one because polls showed him as a Democratic front runner within striking distance of President Bush. In the end, Cuomo declined to enter the race after state budget negotiations stalled.

When Bush went back on his famous "read my lips" promise not to raise taxes, it unmoored an angry Buchanan, who announced his candidacy in December. He did not campaign in Iowa, but his candidacy seemed to be enough to cause the Iowa Republicans to skip the straw poll.

Harkin was flying high coming out of Iowa—he had obliterated the field of contenders, such as it was, by grabbing over 76 percent of the delegate equivalents—only to crash and burn on the granite face of New Hampshire.

1996

THOUGH IOWANS had feared they might lose their first-in-the-nation status following the 1992 election, they were soon reassured when politicians began making pilgrimages to the state not long after President Clinton was inaugurated. In fact, Republican presidential hopeful Lamar Alexander, former governor of Tennessee and the secretary of education under President George H. W. Bush, said in 1995, "There are four ingredients to running for president: money, message, Iowa, and New Hampshire."

The Republicans entered this election cycle energized by their dramatic gains in the 1994 midterm elections. Iowa, too, saw a Republican resurgence, with Terry Branstad defeating Democrat Bonnie Campbell in the governor's race and Republicans taking all five congressional seats. The state economy had improved and noneconomic social issues came to the fore as social conservatives—including Christian evangelicals—increased their influence in the state. In addition, President Clinton was running for reelection unopposed, so all of the caucus action occurred on the Republican side.

Eleven men ran for the nomination, with Kansas senator Bob Dole the early favorite. Texas senator Phil Gramm, former Tennessee governor and secretary of education Lamar Alexander, conservative commentator and hard-liner Pat Buchanan, Pennsylvania senator Arlen Specter, Indiana senator Richard Lugar, businessman Maurice Taylor, former US diplomat and radio talk show host Alan Keyes, California congressman Bob Dornan, California governor Pete Wilson, and businessman Steve Forbes. Dole eventually won the most votes, with Buchanan and Alexander unexpectedly taking second and third. In the fall, Clinton won reelection.

Iowa barely had a chance to clean up from one election cycle before the hordes invaded the state again.

The Louisiana GOP's decision to move its caucus date ahead of Iowa's had Iowa Republican leaders seeing red—Tabasco red.

With the public sick and tired of the intransience of both major parties, the idea of a third party was appealing, especially if someone like retired four-star general and former head of the Joint Chiefs of Staff Colin Powell were to show interest in leading it.

The way campaign laws were rigged, creating a new national party—as businessman and former presidential candidate Ross Perot envisioned—would be a high hurdle to clear. And he could not expect the major parties in Congress to help remove the obstacles.

Powell had all of the qualities requisite to becoming president with only one exception: the desire for the job.

Forbes steamrolled into Iowa fueled by a $440 million fortune. In the last three months of 1995, he outspent front runner Dole by $5.6 million. His key proposal was a flat 17 percent income tax.

One of Forbes's first television ads introduced his main campaign theme, the flat tax. The ad went something like this: "The words that rule our lives. . . : the Declaration of Independence: 1,300 words; the Bible, the Word of God: 773,00 words; the tax code, the words of politicians: 7 million and growing. . . We need to scrap it and replace it with a simple, flat $36,000 tax—free for a family of four." No one can remember where he stood on other issues anymore.

The voters were assaulted with nonstop television ads, most of them negative. Leading the attack was Steve "Free Spending" Forbes, who unleashed $12.5 million in ads and radio spots. The other candidates were compelled to follow suit, spending about ten times more than they had in 1992.

Forbes ultimately spent $37.4 million of his own money in his attempt to become the Republican nominee.

Pat Buchanan, bridge burner extraordinaire. This conservative commentator took a notoriously isolationist approach to trade and immigration.

The race end was as decisive as a flip of the coin. That close.

Following the caucuses, Iowa abruptly returns to its normal broadcasting.

2000

IN 1999, the Republican National Committee enacted new rules intended to prevent the states from jockeying to go first in the caucus/primary schedule: no state could hold a nominating event prior to February 1, and all states had to certify their caucus or primary date by July 1, 1999. This put the Republicans at odds with the Democrats, who mandated a March 1 start, protecting the special status of Iowa and New Hampshire. Those two states responded to efforts to preempt their events by moving them up, regardless of party rules.

Among the Democrats, several potential candidates visited Iowa but ultimately declined to run, leaving the field to former Tennessee senator and current vice president Al Gore, and former professional basketball player and former New Jersey senator Bill Bradley. Gore swamped his rival at the caucuses, earning 63 percent of delegates.

The Republican contest was more crowded, featuring former secretary of education and former Tennessee governor Lamar Alexander, former Family Research Council president Gary Bauer, Ohio congressman John Kasich, businessman Steve Forbes, former US diplomat Alan Keyes, former vice president and former Indiana senator Dan Quayle, New Hampshire senator Bob Smith, former secretary of labor and former American Red Cross president Elizabeth Dole, Missouri senator John Ashcroft, Arizona senator John McCain, conservative commentator Pat Buchanan, Utah senator Orrin Hatch, and Texas governor George W. Bush. Bush, the early favorite, won the caucuses ahead of surprisingly strong finishes by Forbes and Keyes.

The November election ended in a deadlock between Bush and Gore, a virtual tie ultimately decided by the US Supreme Court.

The Cajun Crustacean was at it again in 2000—trying to preempt Iowa's and New Hampshire's first-in-the-nation events despite changes in Republican Party rules intended to prevent such leap-frogging. Iowa House Speaker Brent Siegrist of Council Bluffs had two words for the candidates planning to head to Louisiana: "Phil Gramm." The previous election cycle, Texas senator Gramm had said, "To become president of the United States, I have to win here in Louisiana." Pat Buchanan beat him, and he never recovered.

For the third time, the Republicans had a Dole running for president. This time it was Elizabeth Dole. She challenged the men's exclusive hold on the nation's highest office when she threw her hat in the ring on July 1, 1999.

The Democratic field came down to a one-on-one contest between Bradley and Gore. From the outset it looked like a total mismatch, but Iowa has proven that sitting vice presidents do not always do well here.

Bush, the Republican front runner, said very little during the months before the caucuses. His handlers subscribed to Mark Twain's philosophy that "it's better to keep your mouth shut and appear stupid than open it and remove all doubt." He removed some of the doubt when he commented on the crisis in the Balkans, "I define the [United States and NATO] mission as to restoring Kosovo so the Kosovians can move back in. . ." Calling those who lived in Kosovo "Kosovians" is like calling people who live in Iowa "Iowegians."

With a lead in the polls as big as Texas, Bush was thinking maybe he could just phone it in. Instead of campaigning in Iowa in early 1999, he invited several Iowa Republican legislators to visit him in Texas.

By the time Bush showed up to campaign in June, his Republican rivals were already active in the state. Left to right: Smith, Forbes, Alexander, Buchanan, Dole, Quayle (never a good speller), and Keyes.

Bush spun around $800,000 in campaign cash into a first place showing in the Ames Straw Poll with 7,418 votes.

The other Republican candidates struggled to get into the game, and some in the group were digging their way to China. Left to right, Bauer, Quayle, Forbes, Kasich, McCain, Buchanan, and Keyes.

Bush had raised a whopping $37 million in the first six months of the year, compared to Forbes' largely self-financed $9.4 million and McCain's $6.3 million. Bush's father, former president George H. W. Bush, had coined the phrase "Big Mo"—as in big momentum—when he beat Reagan in the 1980 Iowa Precinct caucuses. Junior's "Big Mo" would take him much further.

In August 1999, the Ames Straw Poll attracted tremendous attention. The participating candidates go to great lengths to buy as many votes as possible. Let's say you have nothing going on the day of the straw poll, and maybe you're a little short on cash but still want to party. Well, my friend, you are in luck—there are a number of politicians who will send a bus to pick you up, pay your entrance fee, feed you, entertain you with a live band, give you free stuff, and give you a ride home, and all you have to do is vote for them (maybe even a couple of times). And the hundreds of reporters who cover this quasi-election go to such great lengths to pretend that it truly means something that people start believing that it really does.

When it was discovered that Gore was soliciting campaign contributions from inside the White House, he said that he hadn't done anything wrong and wouldn't do it again.

Ross Perot's Reform Party held its national convention in Dearborn, Michigan, to nominate its presidential candidate. There was only one problem: none of the named candidates wanted to run. Here: Buchanan, Minnesota governor and former professional wrestler Jesse Ventura, former Connecticut governor Lowell Weicker, and real estate developer Donald Trump.

These gushers of cash were plugged in March 2002 when Bush signed a campaign finance reform bill just before he headed out for a fundraising trip.

Trump considered running for president as the Reform Party candidate but changed his mind when he discovered that he would have to shake hands and kiss babies.

That's the problem with being first: you're always looking over your shoulder (or straight up, in this case). When New Hampshire announced it would hold its primary election on February 1, Iowa officials were compelled to move the caucuses to January 24 to comply with state law even though this move violated both parties' rules.

Bradley's surge in the New Hampshire polls brought out the trash talker in Gore.

George W. Bush announced he was going to run as a "compassionate conservative." Republican hard-liners weren't sure what that was, but they didn't like the sound of it and preferred the fire-breathing Buchanan.

After spending $69 million of his own money on two runs for the White House, Forbes—or his family—put his checkbook away.

The extraordinarily close result of the 2000 election came down to a highly controversial recount in Florida, when ordinary Americans first learned what a "hanging chad" was.

The Supreme Court decided the closest presidential election in history on December 12, when it ruled that the recounts now under way in select Florida counties had to stop because officials were using conflicting standards. The vote was seven to two. The final vote totals showed that Bush won Florida by 537 votes out of approximately 6 million cast and garnered 271 electoral votes — one more than the majority needed to win.

2004

THE IMPACT OF the September 11, 2001 attacks and the resulting wars in Afghanistan and Iraq made national security and international issues more prominent than domestic issues in this caucus cycle. President George W. Bush's declining approval ratings and Democrats' view that his election in 2000 was illegitimate encouraged many to challenge him in 2004.

Democrats began campaigning in Iowa not long after Bush's inauguration in January 2001. The candidates included North Carolina senator John Edwards, Massachusetts senator John Kerry, Missouri congressman Dick Gephardt, Connecticut senator Joe Lieberman, Vermont governor Howard Dean, activist the Reverend Al Sharpton, Ohio congressman Dennis Kucinich, former Illinois senator Carol Moseley Braun, Florida senator Bob Graham, and four-star general Wesley Clark. Though Dean was the early front runner, in the end Kerry won the caucuses with Edwards close behind and Dean a disappointingly distant third. Dean's infamous "I have a scream" concession speech permanently undermined his candidacy. No Republican challenged Bush for the party's nomination in Iowa.

In November, Bush defeated Kerry and returned for a second term in the White House.

Iowans suspect any politician (here, former New Jersey senator Bill Bradley and John Kerry) who shows up in the state shortly after the last election of having ulterior motives.

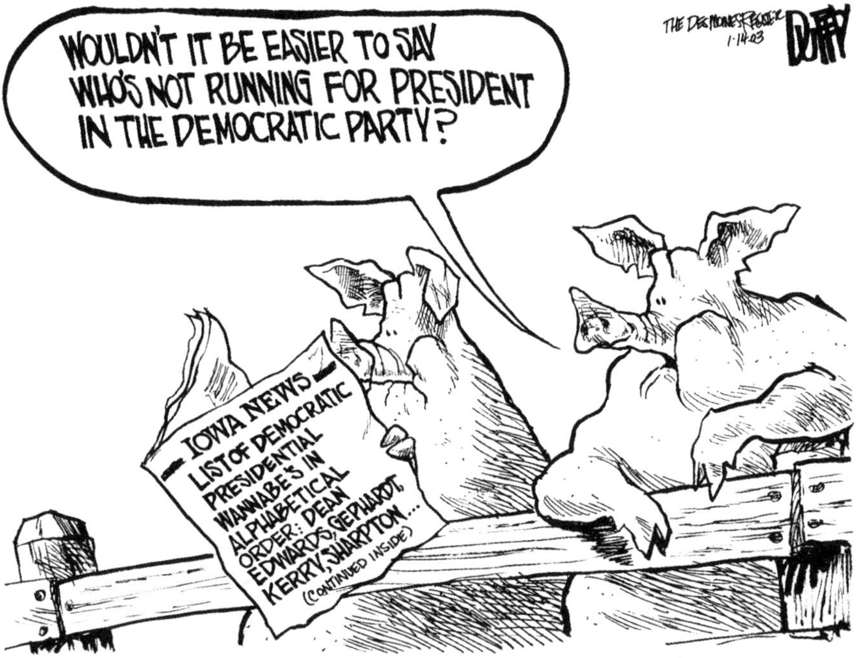

The Democratic field was crowded at the start of the campaign.

Austrian immigrant, action movie star, and California governor Arnold Schwarzenegger gave such a moving keynote speech at the Republican national convention that he overshadowed the candidates and sparked discussion of eliminating the constitutional requirement that presidential candidates be native-born. Left to right: Gephardt, Kucinich, Edwards, Kerry, Dean, and Graham.

Dean's off-the-cuff remarks hurt his campaign for the Democratic nomination.

Iowa senator Tom Harkin's steak fry at the hot air balloon grounds is a mandatory stop for all the Democratic candidates. This year, former president Bill Clinton's keynote speech got all the coverage, leaving the candidates stuck in the mud.

Into an already crowded pool of candidates parachuted General Wesley Clark. From left: Kerry, Graham, Sharpton, Kucinich, Edwards, Gephardt, Dean, Lieberman, and Moseley Braun.

Democratic front runner Dean was beaten up by his rivals, particularly for his positions on taxes, Medicare, and Social Security.

Many candidates are well known, but for various reasons don't connect with Iowans and disappear even before their campaigns get off ground. This was the case for Bob Graham.

Both Lieberman and General Clark decided to focus on New Hampshire and did little campaigning in Iowa; such candidates usually don't succeed.

Dean's famous gaffe—saying he wanted support from everyone, including the guys with confederate flags on their pickups—gave the Reverend Sharpton and others the opportunity to take him to task for racial insensitivity, which hurt him in the polls.

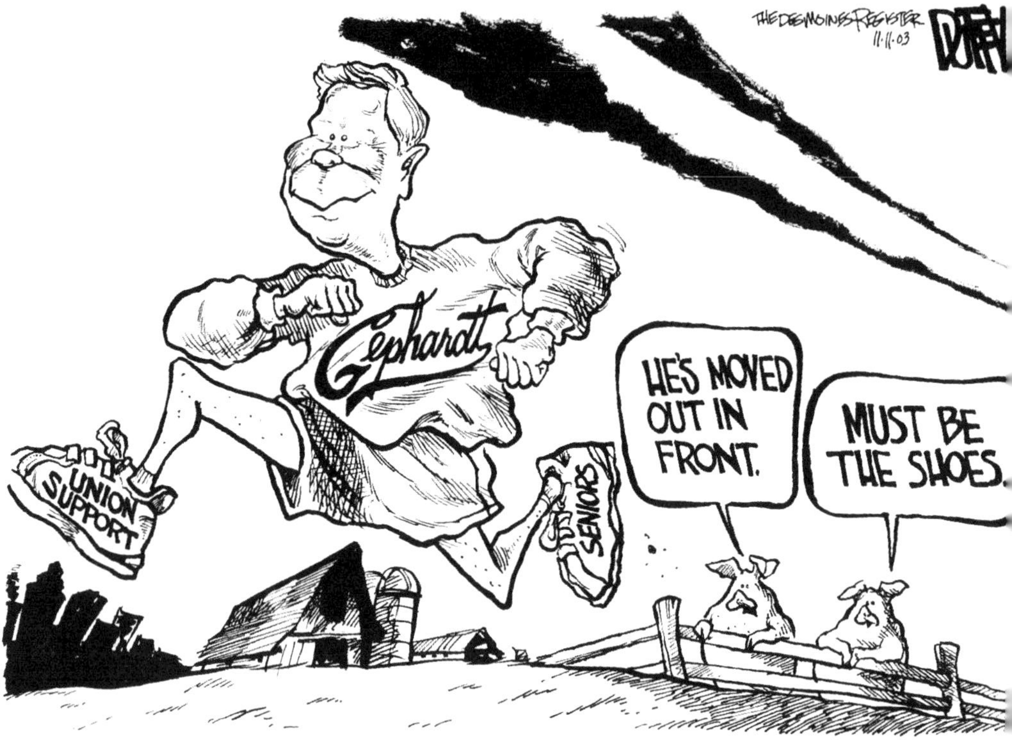

In his third run for president, Gephardt led attacks against Democratic front runner Dean, and with support from seniors and the unions (who supported his free trade platform) he passed Dean in polls.

Dean brought in about 3,500 supporters—mostly young people who wore orange ski caps against the cold and were known as "Deaniacs"—to campaign for him. Billed as a "perfect storm," this labor force overwhelmed those of other candidates.

At one of the candidate forums, the other candidates attacked Dean for his remark about the Confederate flag, forcing him to say he had misspoken.

Harkin's endorsement was crucial for Democrats. Eventually, he endorsed Dean.

The top three candidates (Kerry, Dean, and Gephardt) were so focused on battling each other that they never saw tortoise Edwards sneaking up on them. Edwards ended up in second place with 32.57 delegate equivalents.

At the Black and Brown forum, Dean was attacked again for his racially insensitive remarks. Civil rights activist the Reverend Sharpton asked the governor if he had any blacks or Latinos in his administration, and Dean had to say no. From this point on, he had lost the front runner position.

The final poll before the caucuses showed four candidates neck-and-neck: Gephardt, Dean, Kerry, and Edwards.

The infamous "Dean scream" howled into American history on the night of the caucuses, when Dean came in third. His surprised staff had not prepared a concession speech, leaving him to improvise.

2008

PRESIDENT BUSH's very low approval ratings and Democrats' success in the 2006 midterm elections made Democrats enthusiastic and Republicans glum about this election cycle. With neither a sitting president nor vice president running, the field was open in both parties.

Republicans who threw their hat into the ring included Arizona senator John McCain, former New York City mayor Rudy Giuliani, Kansas senator Sam Brownback, former Massachusetts governor Mitt Romney, former Arkansas governor and Southern Baptist preacher Mike Huckabee, former Tennessee senator Fred Thompson, Colorado congressman Tom Tancredo, former Virginia governor Jim Gilmore, former Wisconsin governor Tommy Thompson, California congressman Duncan Hunter, Illinois businessman John Cox, and Texas congressman Ron Paul. Iowa's social and religious conservatives exercised considerable influence in this caucus cycle and ultimately gave Huckabee the nod, with national front runner Romney coming in second and Thompson third; eventual presidential nominee McCain came in fourth.

Democratic candidates included the early front runner New York senator Hillary Clinton, former North Carolina senator John Edwards, Illinois senator Barack Obama, New Mexico governor Bill Richardson, Connecticut senator Chris Dodd, Delaware senator Joe Biden, Ohio congressman

Dennis Kucinich, former Alaska senator Mike Gravel, and former Iowa governor Tom Vilsack. Obama, initially thought to be a second-tier candidate, eventually topped the caucuses with Edwards barely beating former front runner Clinton.

In the fall, Obama defeated McCain to make history as the United States' first African American president. He was also one of only three non-incumbent candidates, (along with Jimmy Carter and George W. Bush) to win both the Iowa caucuses and the White House.

The Democratic Party did not want a rerun of 2004, when Massachusetts senator John Kerry snatched defeat from the jaws of victory in his campaign against Bush.

Edwards parlayed his second-place finish in the 2004 Iowa caucuses into the vice-presidential slot for that year's election. Returning to Iowa shortly after the Kerry/Edwards ticket was defeated, Edwards built on the foundation he had laid earlier. However, early national polls showed him trailing his old running mate, Hillary Clinton.

A statewide poll showed that Edwards was the new choice of 30 percent of Iowa Democrats, with Clinton at 26 percent, Kerry at 12 percent, and Vilsack at 10 percent. Edwards had visited the state twenty-six times between 2005 and July of 2007, hitting all ninety-nine counties, and it paid off.

Some Iowans found the prospect of a second Clinton presidency—after two Presidents Bush—unappetizing. Former first lady and mother of a president Barbara Bush said in 2014, "If we can't find more than two or three families to run for high office, that's silly. . . The Kennedys, Clintons, Bushes—there are just more families than that."

Politicians found wandering about Iowa in the dead of winter are understood to have ulterior motives for their presence.

Obama in the mode of the famous painting of George Washington crossing the Delaware during the American Revolution. Instead of the Delaware, it was the Mississippi, and instead of the Hessians, he faced the entrenched forces of leading candidates Clinton and Edwards.

The 2008 presidential election opened the floodgates and the prospective candidates came pouring into the state. This was the first time since 1952 that they had neither a sitting president nor a vice president to contend with. A total of thirty prospective candidates visited Iowa in the months leading up to the caucuses.

When Adlai Stevenson ran for president in the 1950s, he was famous for wearing out his shoes on the campaign trail. Biden unloaded this .45 slug through his size 10s by saying in reference to Barack Obama, "I mean, you got the first mainstream African American who is articulate and bright and clean and a nice-looking guy. I mean, that's a storybook, man."

The decision by the Florida Republicans to move their primary date up caused a chain-reaction pileup as the states that traditionally held the early caucuses and primaries rushed to stay first.

Eventually, Iowa conservatives judged Huckabee "just right." Mainstream Republicans lacked the fire-and-brimstone seasoning that the evangelicals were looking for.

Vilsack failed to raise the money he needed for a competitive presidential bid.

Clinton's tortured explanation of her evolving positions on ethanol.

The Arizona senator fired up his all-new Straight Talk Express bus on a campaign swing through Iowa, telling reporters, "My positions haven't changed, I'm too old to change. I'm the same. People will understand that as the campaign goes on." He forgot that he came out against ethanol subsidies back in 2000 but now supported them.

The Iowa Poll released in early December showed Obama sprinting past a faltering Clinton, who had slipped four points since the last poll was released in early November.

Romney had a tough time running away from the fact that he had changed his positions on everything from health care to abortion.

Iowa Republicans set January 3 as the date of their presidential caucuses, leaving New Hampshire as the only early-voting state without a firm date for its nominating contest.

Major candidates Giuliani and McCain chose to bypass the Iowa Straw Poll, leaving Romney as the only top-tier candidate to participate. In the long run, the decision had no negative effect on either campaign. McCain went on to become the GOP nominee, while Giuliani's campaign burned up in the Florida sun.

McCain had been considered the front runner ever since he declared his intention to seek the presidency, but in reality his campaign was headed to an early grave. It was plagued by staff dissention and was virtually broke, so McCain went "underground" in an attempt to recover. He reappeared in mid-September with a slimmed-down campaign apparatus and headed off to Waterloo, Iowa, for the start of what the campaign called the No Surrender Tour.

The Grinnell College newspaper reported that Clinton's campaign had fed a student a question to ask the candidate at an event in Newton, Iowa. The Grinnell student said that a Clinton staffer produced a series of questions from a binder and asked if she'd like to ask Hillary a specific question on her energy plan. It was reported that the student was not the only one to be fed questions.

Article 6 of the Constitution states that "no religious test shall ever be required as a qualification to any office or public trust under the United States," yet there were evangelicals in Iowa who said they could not vote for Romney because he is a member of the Church of Latter-Day Saints. His chief rival in Iowa at the time was Mike Huckabee, who was quoted by a *New York Times* reporter as asking, "Don't Mormons believe that Jesus and the devil are brothers?"

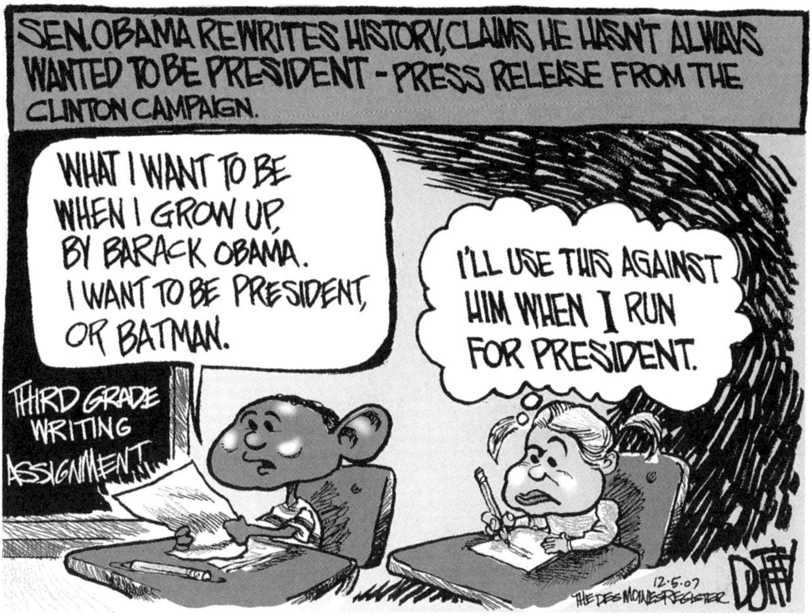

Clinton's staff stumbled across a remark made by one of Obama's teachers in Indonesia about an essay he had written in kindergarten. When asked what he wanted to be when he grew up, he wrote that he wanted to become president. The Clinton folks promptly warned the American people: "Senator Obama Rewrites History, Claims He Hasn't Been Planning White House Run. . . Senator Obama's comment today is fundamentally at odds with what his teachers, family, classmates, and staff have said about his plans to run for President. Senator Obama's campaign rhetoric is getting in the way of his reality."

All of the major candidates led in the polls at one point or another, and up until the caucuses, many voters indicated they were still undecided.

Fred Thompson got off to a very slow start in the state. With just two weeks to go before the Iowa caucuses, he was still a mystery to many Iowa voters. A last-minute fifty city bus tour was a case of too little, too late.

Hillary Clinton's campaign spent $29 million in her effort to win the Iowa caucuses. She came in third behind Obama and Edwards. There was talk that she left one of her greatest assets chained to the porch too long.

2012

INCUMBENT PRESIDENT Barack Obama ran unopposed on the Democratic side; among Republicans, the nomination was hotly contested. Once again Iowa's religious and social conservatives played an outsize role in producing a result that national commentators declared unrepresentative of the nation.

The Republican candidates included former Utah governor Jon Huntsman Jr., former Minnesota governor Tim Pawlenty, businessman Herman Cain, former Alaska governor Sarah Palin, Minnesota congresswoman and Tea Party leader Michele Bachmann, Texas governor Rick Perry, former Georgia congressman and former speaker of the house Newt Gingrich, Texas congressman Ron Paul, former Pennsylvania senator Rick Santorum, and the national front runner, former Massachusetts governor Mitt Romney. Initially Romney received the tip, but Iowa Republicans soon had to admit that he had been edged out by a few hundred votes by Santorum. Religious conservatives preferred Santorum to the more moderate Romney, who also suffered from prejudice against his Mormon faith. Paul ran a surprisingly close third.

In the fall, Obama defeated Romney to win reelection.

After bruising battles with Congress, Obama headed out on the campaign trail, parading a million-dollar bus and his entourage over Iowa's rural roads in the hope of reviving the support that helped him win in 2008.

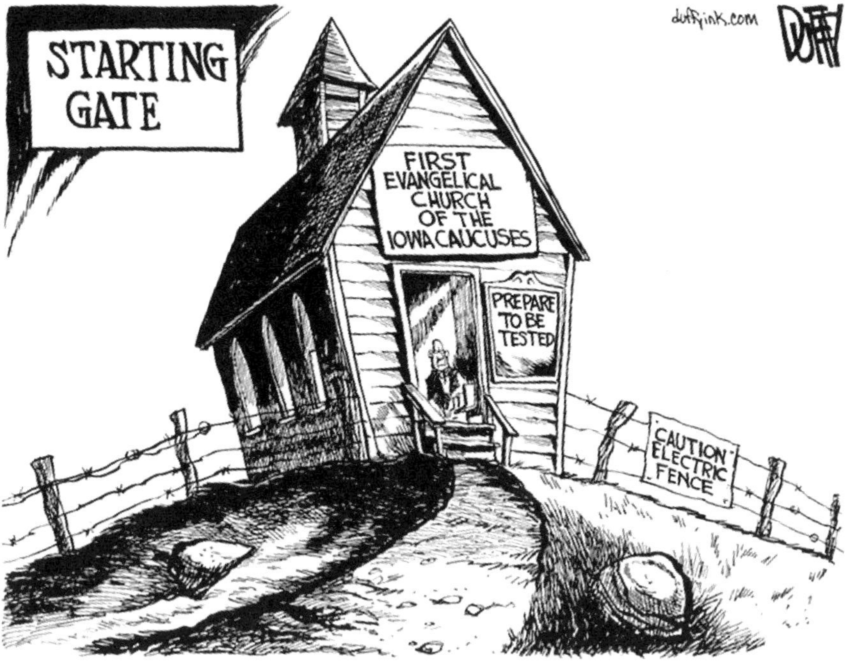

The GOP candidates had to pass a stringent test from Iowa's evangelical political activists if they hoped to succeed in the caucuses.

Gingrich carried some heavy baggage into the 2012 campaign.

Former Minnesota governor Tim Pawlenty was too honest for his own good about one of Iowa's sacred cows.

Perry came to regret calling Social Security a Ponzi scheme, and rival Romney looked to gain the advantage.

Evangelical CEO of the Family Leader, Bob Vander Plaats hoped to have a large role in determining the Republican nominee, usurping the role usually played by Iowa senator Chuck Grassley.

Florida and South Carolina tried to jump the line to hold their Republican presidential polls before the New Hampshire and Iowa events, much to the dismay of the GOP.

Pigs can't fly, especially when their right wing is overloaded. From left to right: Paul, Gingrich, Cain, Pawlenty, Bachmann, Santorum, and Palin. The pilot is Iowa governor Terry Branstad.

The Iowa Republican Party spun straw polls into gold for the party's coffers.

The reported and actual meanings of an Iowa straw poll win, here for Michele Bachmann.

Paul echoes comedian Rodney Dangerfield's best-known line in complaining about national media neglect of his campaign.

Perry famously forgot one of his own major policy proposals, his memory—and his candidacy—as dry and empty as west Texas.

Palin visited Iowa, but whether or not she planned to run for the GOP nomination never became clear.

Real estate developer Donald Trump, famous for his coiffure, always played the Iowa field but never committed.

Cain said on the *Tonight Show* that if he was the "flavor of the week," according to the polls his nickname would be "Black Walnut." His candidacy melted when women began accusing him of sexual harassment.

Iowans expect to see and talk with candidates in person, but in 2012 the GOP candidates spent most of their time in televised debates.

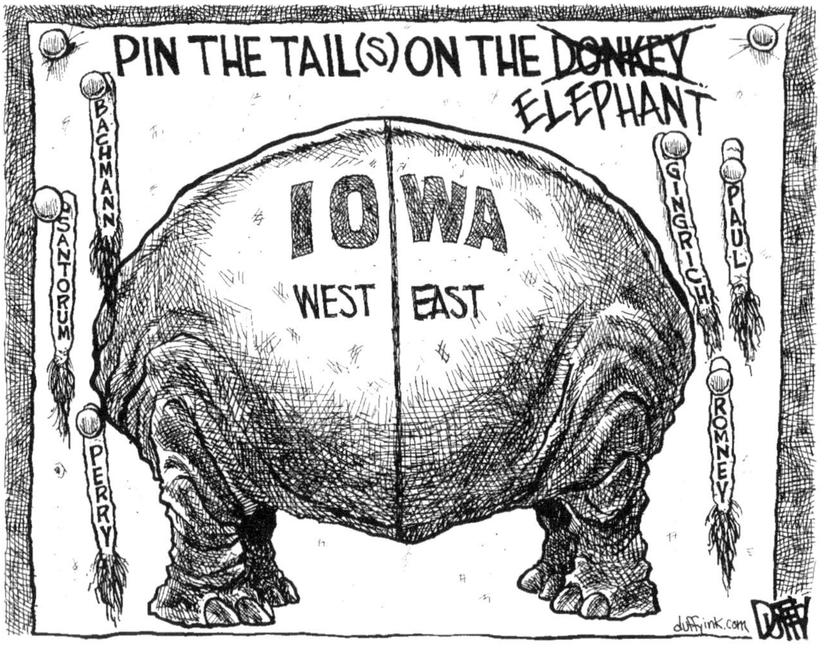

Iowa divides politically down the middle, along I-35, with the west favoring more conservative candidates and the east more moderate ones. The candidates went where they would be most welcome.

Gingrich reached out to Iowa evangelicals in an effort to overcome his poor reputation among them. Left of God, the Reverend Cary Gordon; on the right under God's arm, Bob Vander Plaats.

Iowa state senator Kent Sorenson ingratiated himself with Bachmann's campaign and allegedly enriched himself while serving as her state campaign manager before abruptly switching his support to Paul.

To the annoyance of many Iowans, the GOP race was so close that the campaigning continued through Christmas.

The national media were unable to pick a winner in the GOP race.

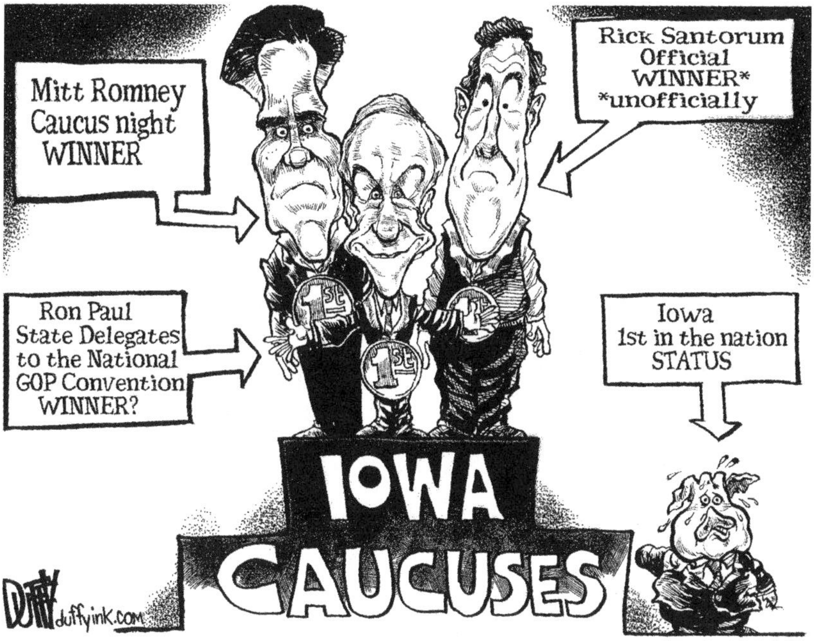

The race was so close it was hard to call, with first Romney and then Santorum being called the winner, while Paul walked away with the most state delegates to the nominating convention. The mess left the Iowa GOP worried for its first-in-the-nation status.

Santorum, a dark horse candidate, invoked the old children's story about a determined railroad engine and campaigned the old-fashioned way by going to all ninety-nine of Iowa's counties.

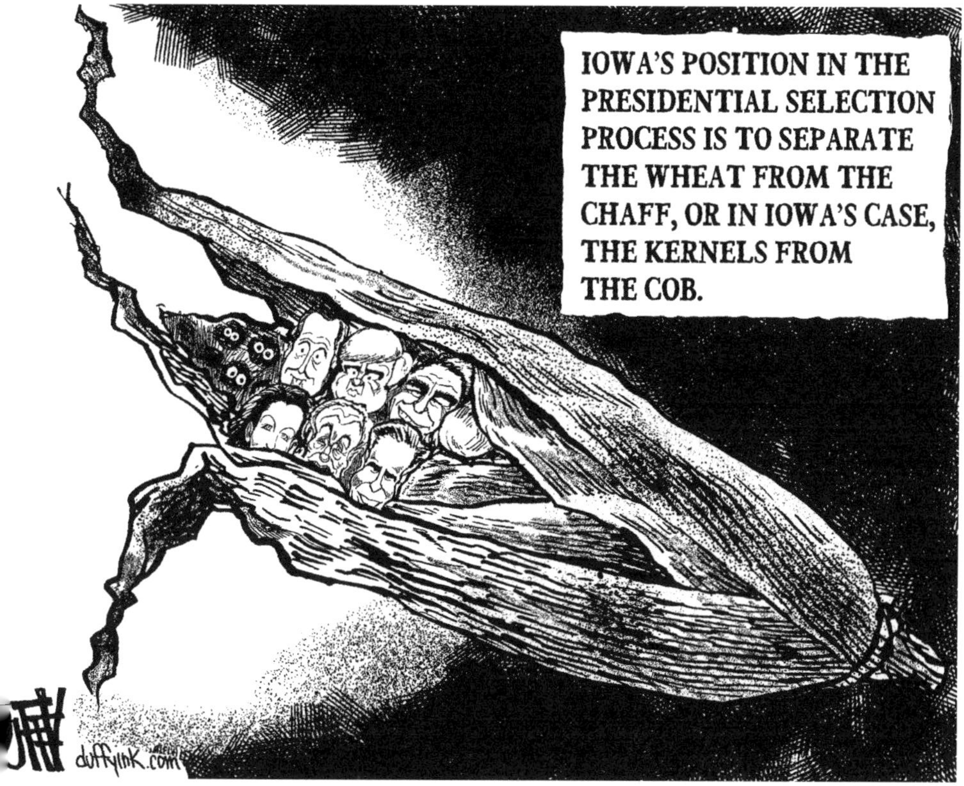

Iowa is the nation's biggest corn-growing state, so its role in the presidential race might best be likened to shucking corn. Top, left to right: Santorum, Gingrich, and Perry; bottom, left to right: Bachmann, Paul, and Romney.

Though Romney had the lead in the GOP race, Paul's supporters dominated Iowa's selection of delegates to the nominating convention. This is what happens when the candidates forget that the caucuses are a four-part process.

Iowa has a squeaky clean reputation politically—or it did until the ethically challenged 2012 caucus cycle.

Iowa has opened the presidential race since 1972, but as a small state, it often doesn't get much attention by the end. The 2012 race between Obama and Romney was so close that Iowa enjoyed visits from the candidates right up to the last minute.

Iowa and the Midwest Experience

Carnival in the Countryside: The History of the Iowa State Fair
By Chris Rasmussen

The Drake Relays: America's Athletic Classic
By David Peterson

Dubuque's Forgotten Cemetery: Excavating a Nineteenth-Century Burial Ground in a Twenty-First Century City
By Robin M. Lillie and Jennifer E. Mack

Duffy's Iowa Caucus Cartoons: Watch 'Em Run
By Brian Duffy

Iowa Past to Present: The People and the Prairie, Revised Third Edition
By Dorothy Schwieder, Thomas Morain, and Lynn Nielsen

The Iowa State Fair
By Kurt Ullrich

The Lost Region: Toward a Revival of Midwestern History
By Jon K. Lauck

Main Street Public Library: Community Places and Reading Spaces in the Rural Heartland, 1876–1956
By Wayne A. Wiegand

Necessary Courage: Iowa's Underground Railroad in the Struggle against Slavery
By Lowell Soike

On Behalf of the Family Farm: Iowa Farm Women's Activism since 1945
By Jenny Barker Devine

A Store Almost in Sight: The Economic Transformation of Missouri from the Louisiana Purchase to the Civil War
By Jeff Bremer

Transcendental Meditation in America: How a New Age Movement Remade a Small Town in Iowa
By Joseph Weber

What Happens Next? Essays on Matters of Life and Death
By Douglas Bauer